DOBRO® Classics Plus

20 CLASSIC AND ORIGINAL TUNES

BY STEVE TOTH

DOBRO CORPORATION, LTD.
MANUFACTURERS
MUSICAL STRING INSTRUMENTS
LOS ANGELES ... CALIFORNIA

This book is dedicated to my mom and dad, Marie and Steve Toth

Dobro is a registered mark of the Gibson Guitar Co.

SAN 683-8022
ISBN 1-57424-022-6

Music Typesetting - Dave Cententano
Cover Photo - Chuck Rausin
Paste-up - Cindy Middlebrook
Layout and Production - Ron Middlebrook

CONTENTS

DOBRO CLASSICS PLUS - CD

INSTRUMENT INFORMATION

TRACK	TUNE	INSTRUMENT MAKE & MODEL	YEAR BUILT*	NECK SHAPE	PAGE
1	Bill Cheathem	Harlow Walnut	1997	Square	6
2	Blackberry Blossom	Dobro Model 27 (Cal.)	1937	Square	8
3	Bugle Call Rag	Dobro Model 55 (Cal.)	1929	Round	10
4	Call Of The Mountains	Scheerhorn Maple L Body	2001	Square	12
5	Daybreak In Dixie	Dobro Model 27 (Regal)	1936	Square	16
6	Dear Old Dixie	Dobro Model 27 Cyclops (Cal.)	1931	Square	18
7	Dixie Hoedown	Dobro Model 45 (Regal)	1936	Square	20
8	Fireball Mail	Dobro Model 27 (Cal.)	1935	Round	22
9	Gold Rush	Dobro Model 65 (Cal.)	1936	Square	23
10	Greensleeves Intro	Dobro Model 45 (Cal.)	1937	Square	25
11	Greensleeves	"	"	"	"
12	Katy Hill	Dobro Model 37 (Cal.)	1936	Square	27
13	Pickaway	Dobro Model 37 (Regal)	1935	Square	29
14	Red Haired Boy	Dobro Model 45 (Regal)	1934	Square	31
15	Sally Ann	**Magno-Tone Double Cyclops(Cal.)**	1929	Round	33
16	Sally Goodin	Dobro Model 27 Deluxe (OMI)	1995	Square	35
17	Salt Creek	Dobro Model 86 (Cal.)	1932	Round	37
18	**Sliding Down The Road Intro**	Wolfe Brazilian Rosewood	1991	Square	39
19	Sliding Down The Road	"	"	"	"
20	Sometimes Alone	Dobro Model 156 (Cal.)	1929	Round	42
21	Southwind	Beard Birch Plywood	1999	Square	44
22	Step To It Intro	Dobro Model 27 (Cal.)	1936	Round	46
23	Step To It	"	"	"	"
24	Call of the Mountains**	Dobro Model 37 (Regal)	1936	Square	
25	**Sliding Down The Road****	"	"	"	
26	Sometimes Alone**	"	"	"	
27	Southwind**	"	"	"	
28	Step To It**	Dobro Model 55 (Cal.)	1929	Round	

* Pre-war dates are approximate

**From CD "Sliding Down The Road"

Stephen Toth's interest in bluegrass and country music grew from roots in the bluegrass and folk sounds of the 50's and early 60's. At the age of 16, he added the dobro to his list of performing instruments which now includes the guitar, five string banjo, pedal steel guitar and bass. The author has recently been performing on the dobro with several bluegrass and country groups in addition to doing recording work. Stephen has a new CD release called "Sliding Down The Road" (see page 47), plus a book/cassette package called "Dobro Techniques, for Bluegrass and Country Music" published by Centerstream Publishing.

Foreword

So - you've been playing the dobro (alias-resophonic guitar) for a while now and you love it! But, you would like to learn some of the early classic instrumentals and more of the tunes that come up in jam sessions.

Well, you have come to the right place!! In this collection of tablatures, I have included many of the tunes I've heard again and again at various jam sessions in all parts of the country (and around the world) and on many recordings. They incorporate lots of the sounds and styles developed by the "masters", and focus primarily on uptempo tunes. In addition, I have included five of my original instrumentals which are on my first solo CD/Cassette "SLIDING DOWN THE ROAD".

One suggestion as you work with the book - although most of the tunes are quite fast when played at normal speed - practice and learn (memorize) a tune slowly (70-80 beats per minute), all the way through, before trying to bring it up to speed. Also, notice that the "hammer-on/pull-off" runs and licks which are in many tunes are tabbed and played in several various ways. These are basically different styles, with slightly different sounds while playing the same notes, which can be used interchangeably once you master the techniques.

Have a sliding-good time!

Steve Toth

Del McCoury and Sons, Ronnie and Robbie with Steve Toth sitting in, August, 1994 Photo: Bob Mavian

4

TABLATURE EXPLAINED

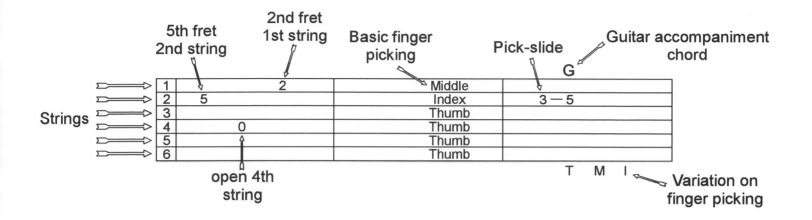

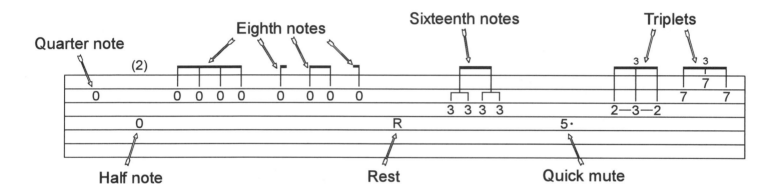

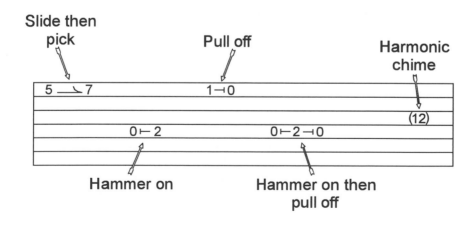

BILL CHEATHEM

key: G

Arranged by Steve Toth

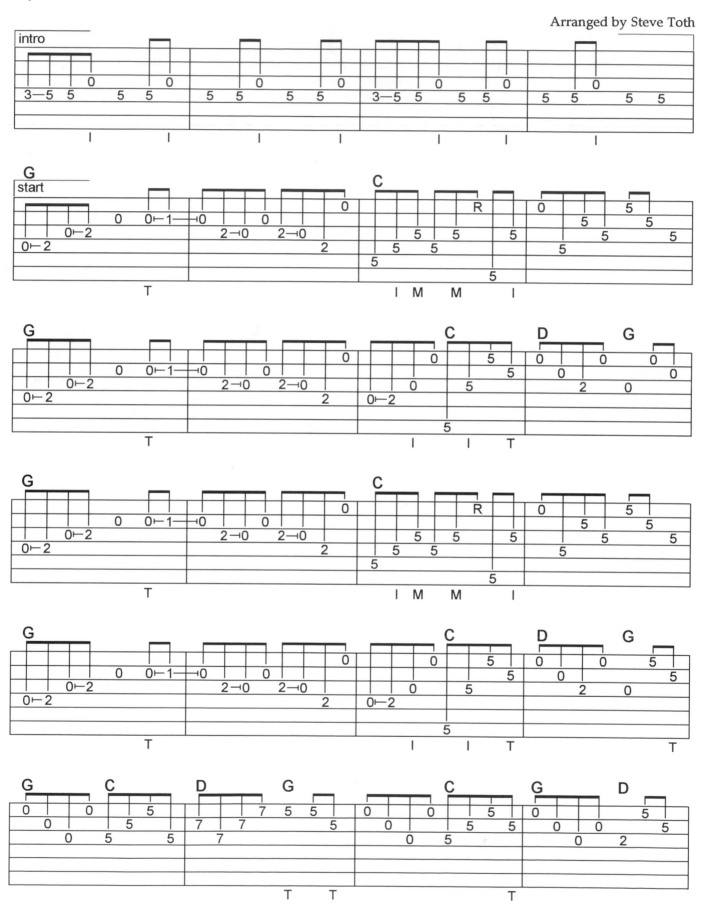

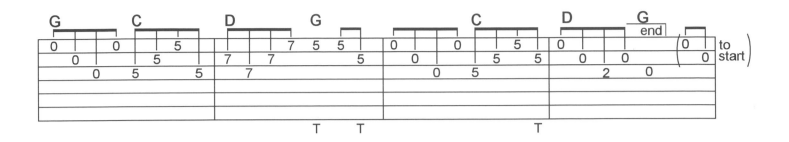

Kathy Barwick

Dobro Model 55 - #1586 - 1929

Dobro Model 55 - #1586 - 1929

BLACKBERRY BLOSSOM

key: G

Arranged by Steve Toth

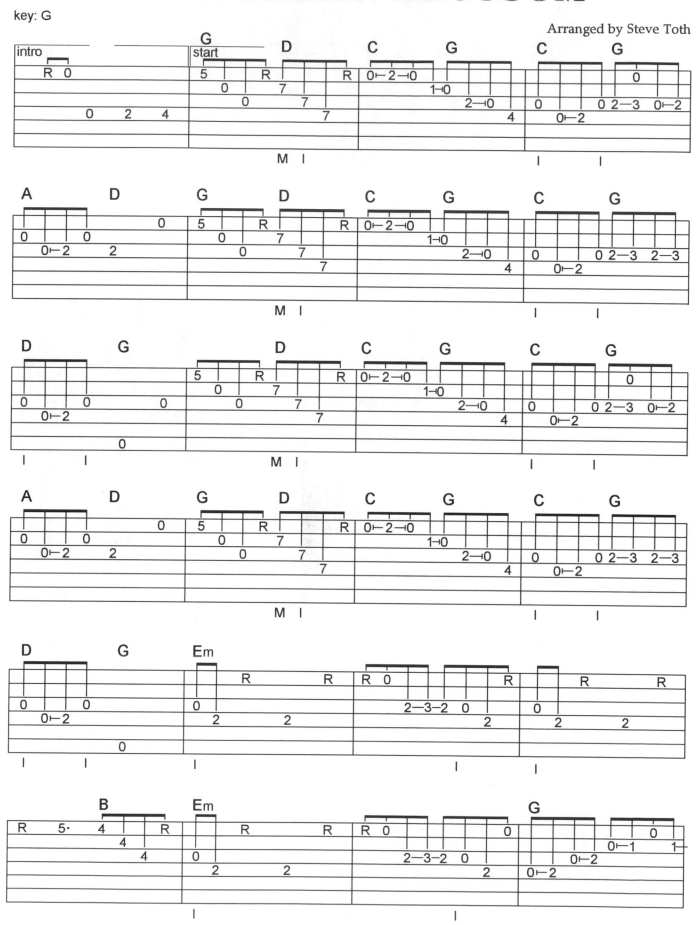

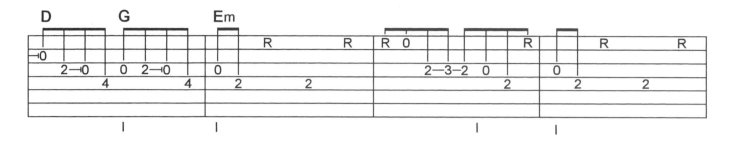

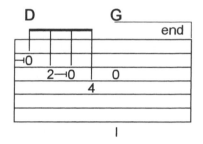

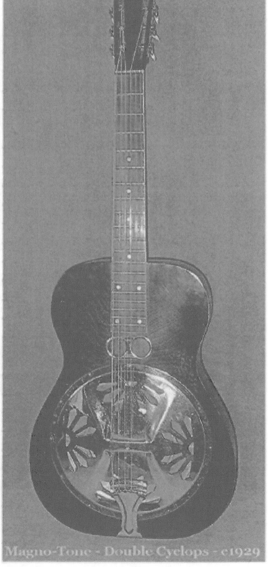

Dobro Model 55 - #116 - 1929   Magno-Tone - Double Cyclops - c1929

BUGLE CALL RAG

J. Pettis, B. Meyers, E. Schoebel
Arranged by Steve Toth

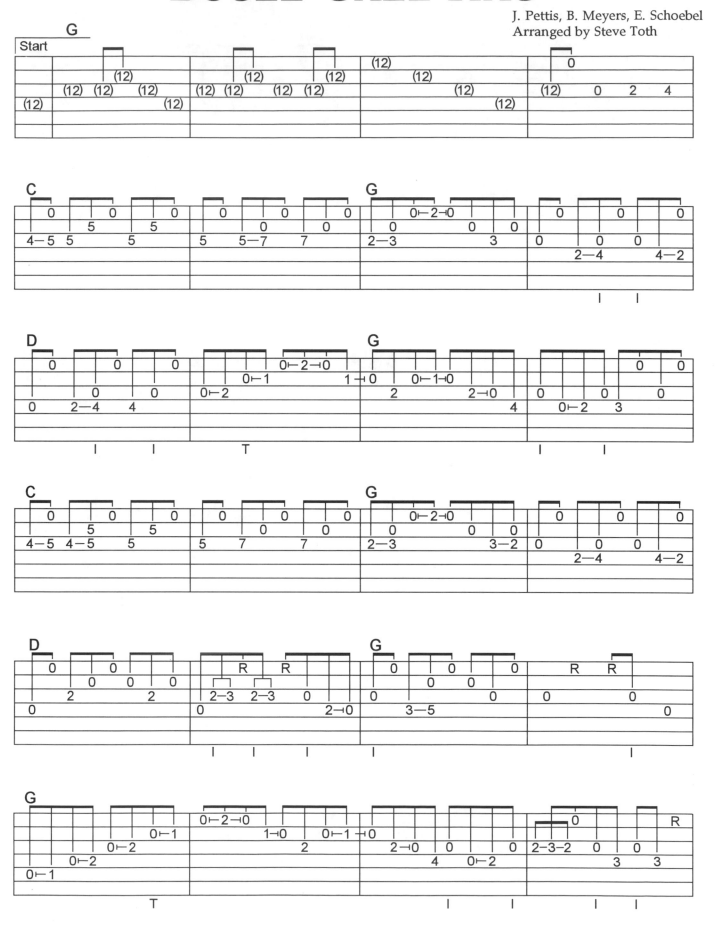

10

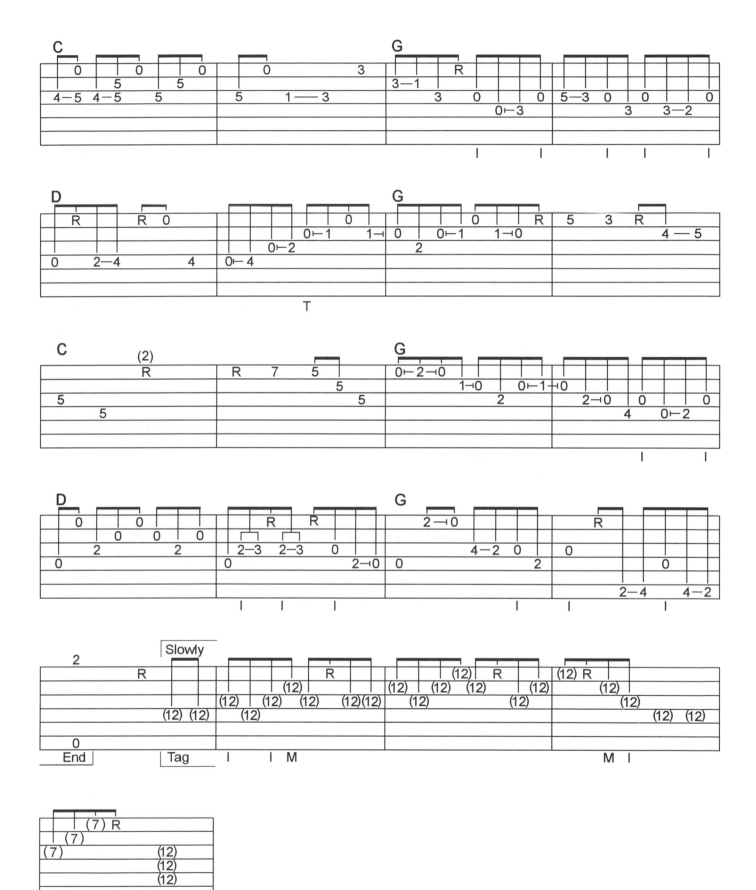

CALL OF THE MOUNTAINS

key: G

by Steve Toth

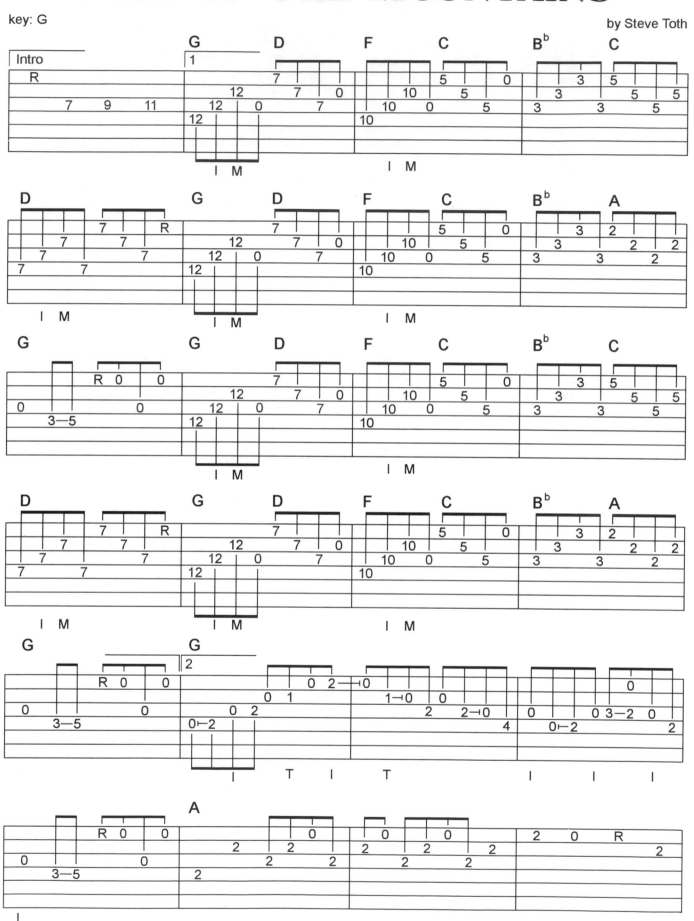

13

Dobro Model 125 Custom - #1780 - 1929

Dobro Model 86 - #2932 2 - 1932

Repeat part one

Bb   A   G

Ending

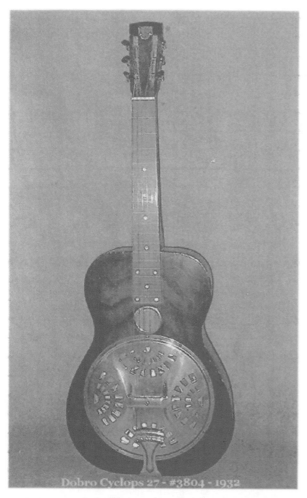

Dobro Cyclops 27 - #3804 – 1932

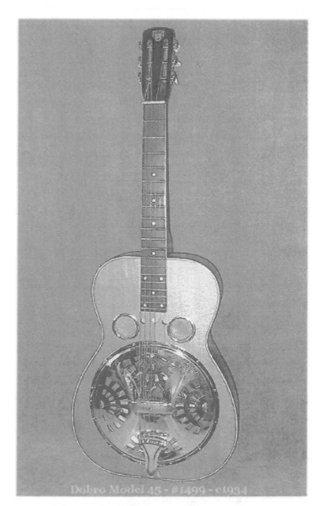

Dobro Model 45 - #1499 - c1934

Dobro Model 27 - #6999 – 1935

Dobro Model 37 - c1936

DAYBREAK IN DIXIE

Bill Napier
Arranged by Steve Toth

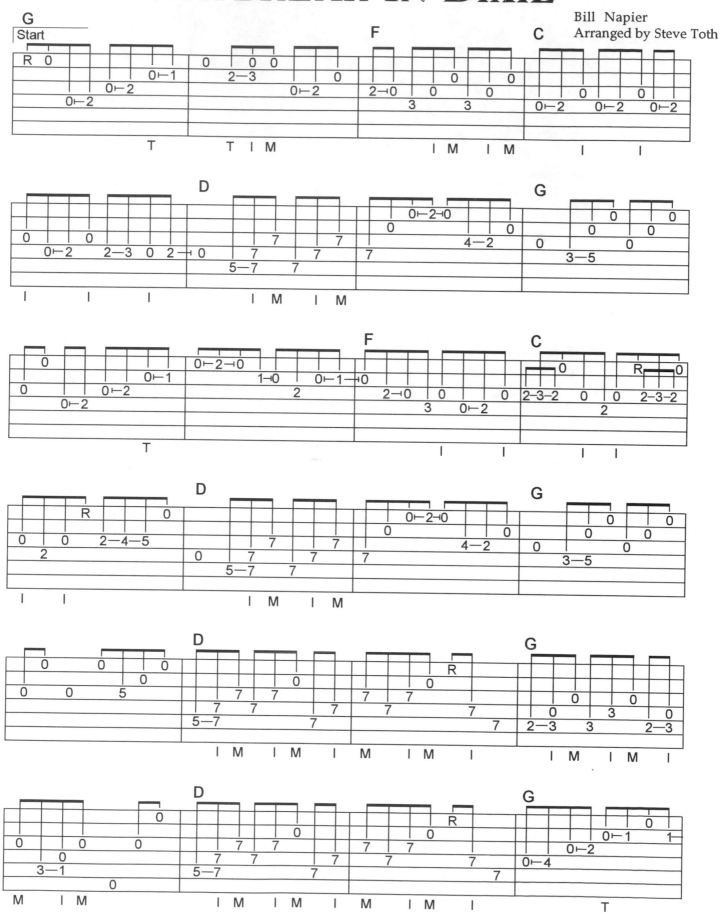

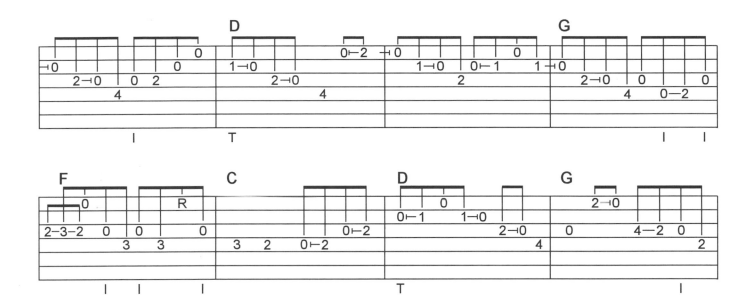

Steve Toth & Rippling River
on stage at the Wind Gap Bluegrass Festival, June, 1995

DEAR OLD DIXIE

Arranged by Steve Toth

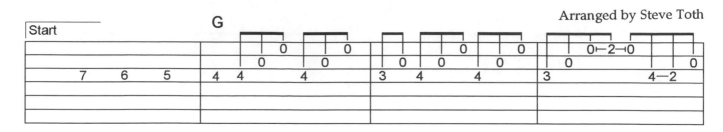

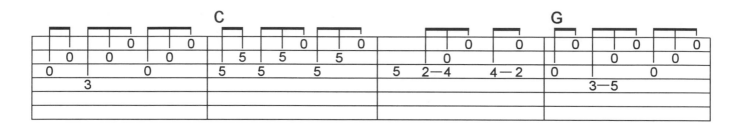

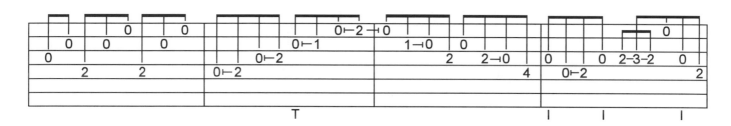

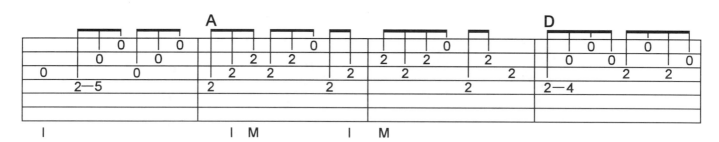

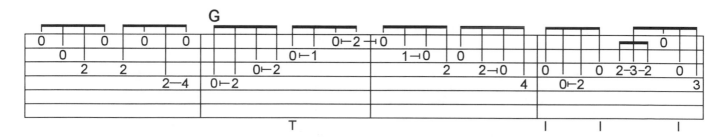

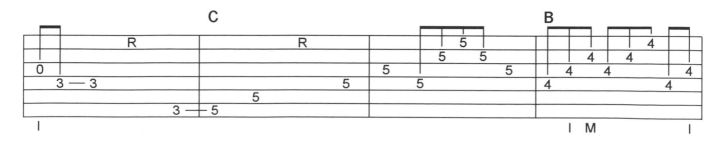

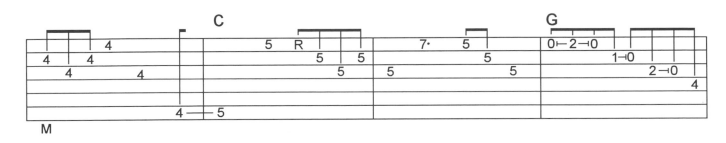

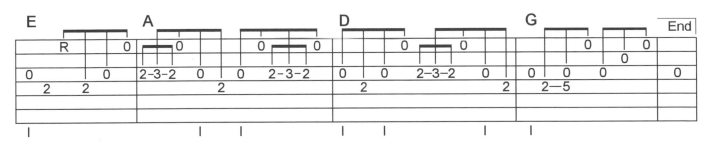

Sally Van Meter

Dobro Model 27 - #7616 – 1936

DIXIE HOEDOWN

J & J McReynolds
Arranged by Steve Toth

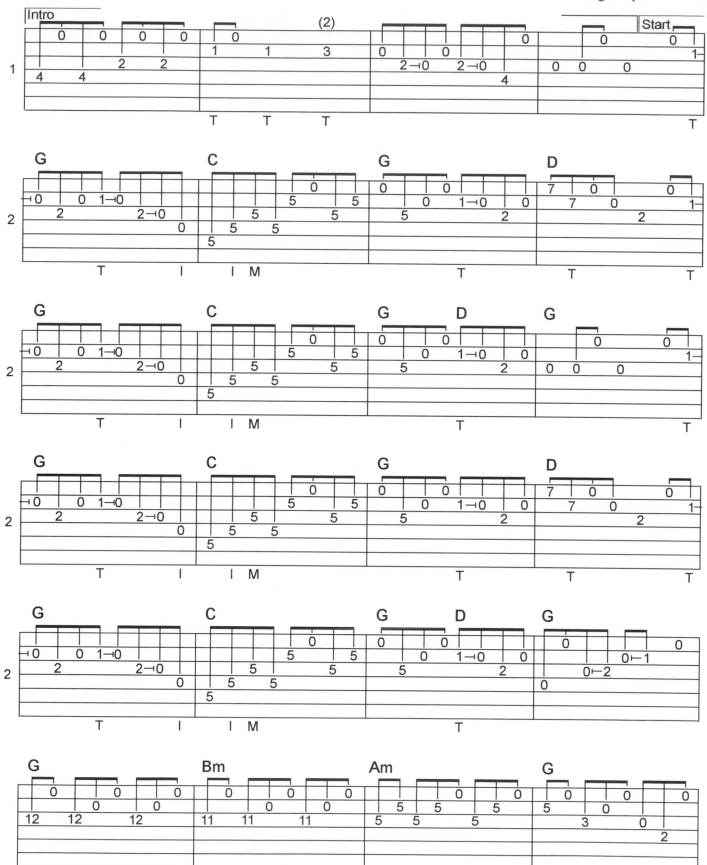

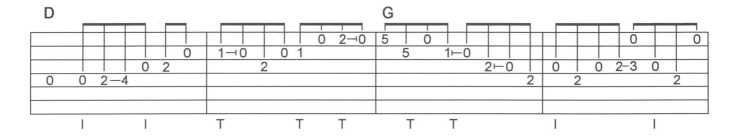

Rome bluegrass group "New Country Kitchen"
with Steve Toth sitting in, Rome, Italy - March,1995
Photo: Louise Toth

Fireball Mail

F. Rose
Arranged by Steve Toth

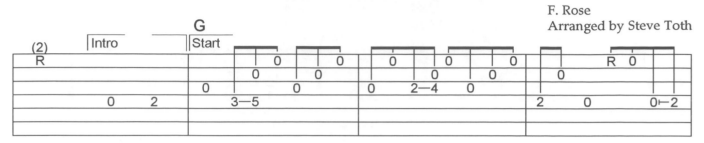

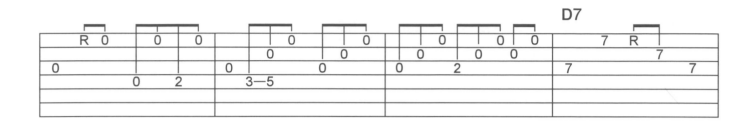

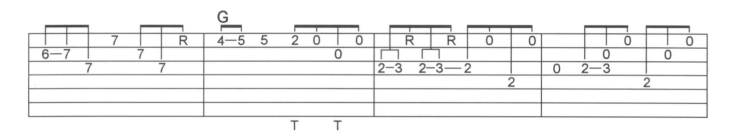

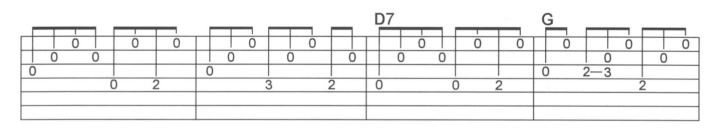

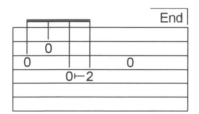

GOLD RUSH

Arranged by Steve Toth

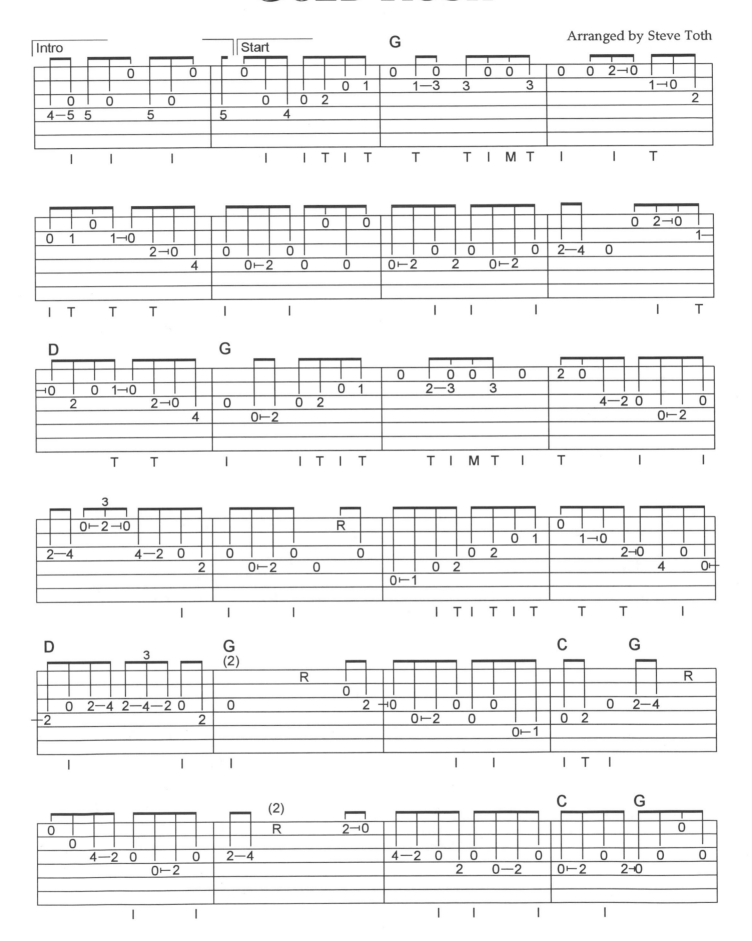

23

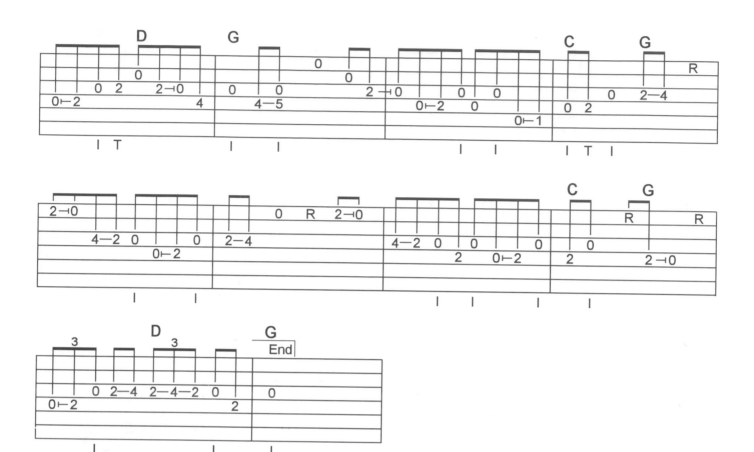

21 of the top dobro players in the world on stage at the 1995
IBMA Music Awards Show in Owensboro, Kentucky, September 21, 1995
Steve Toth is fifth from the left. Tim Scheerhorn is right in the middle, back row with
suit and tie. Sally Van Meter is in there too. Can you recognize any others?

Photo: Brian Barker - Radio MANX - Isle Of Man, British Isles

GREENSLEEVES

Arranged by Steve Toth

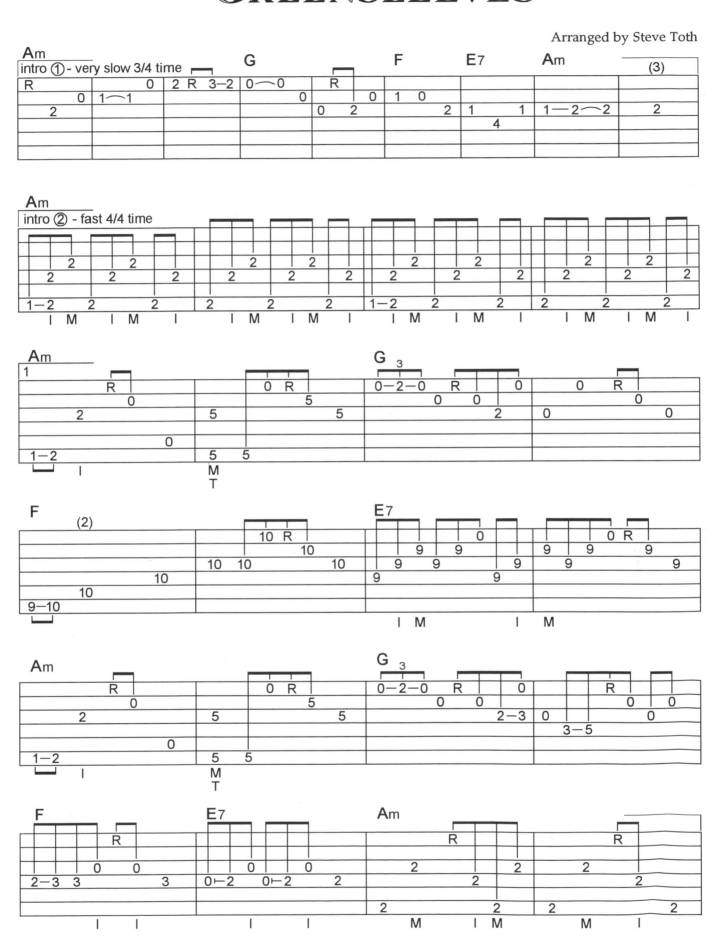

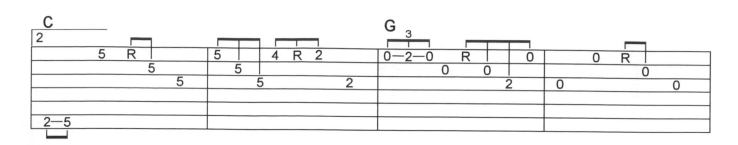

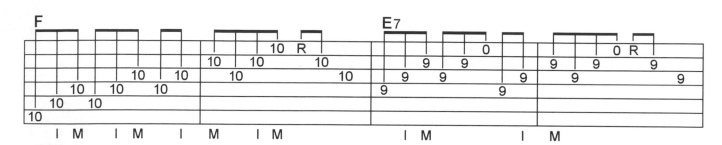

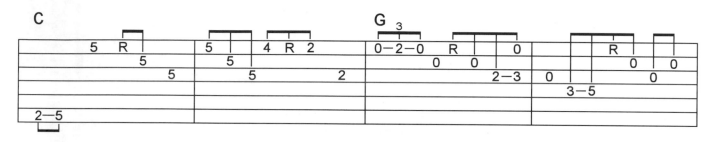

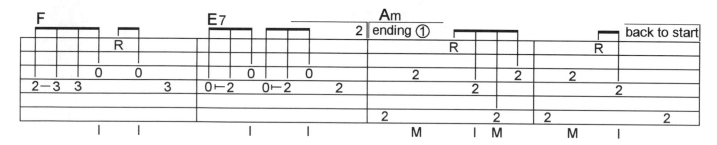

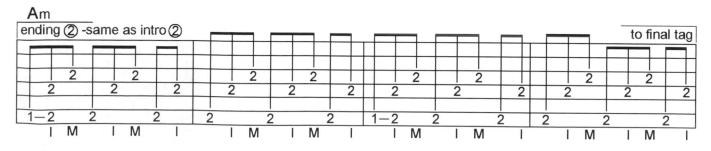

KATY HILL

key: G

Arranged by Steve Toth

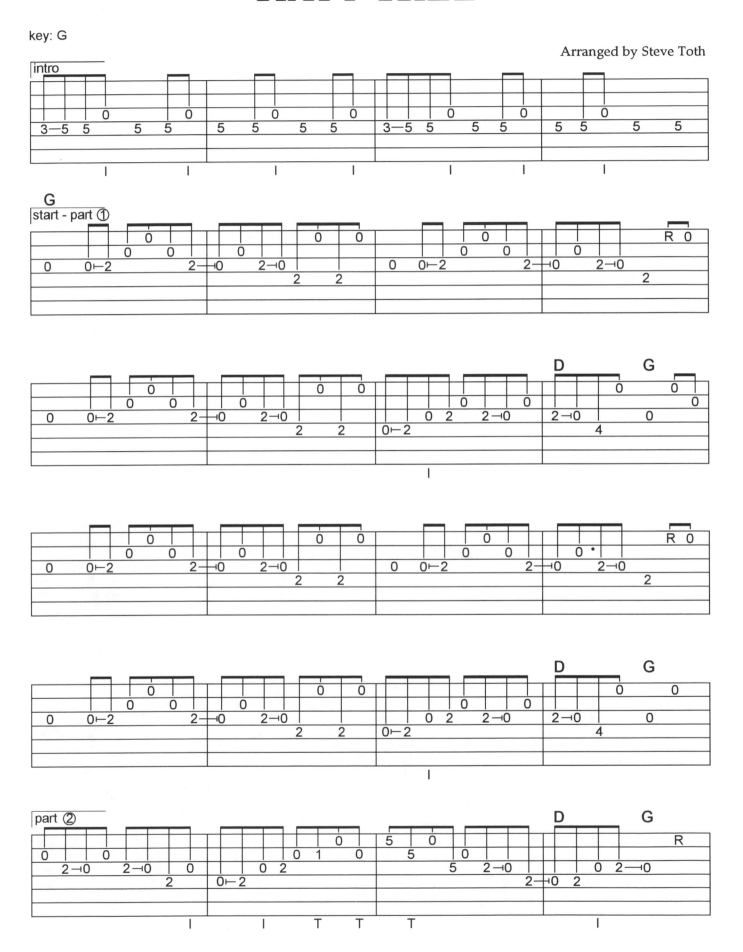

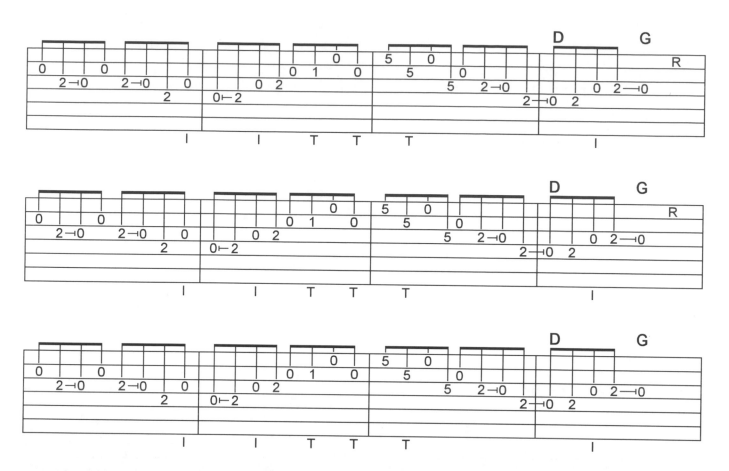

PICKAWAY

Vic Jordan
Arranged by Steve Toth

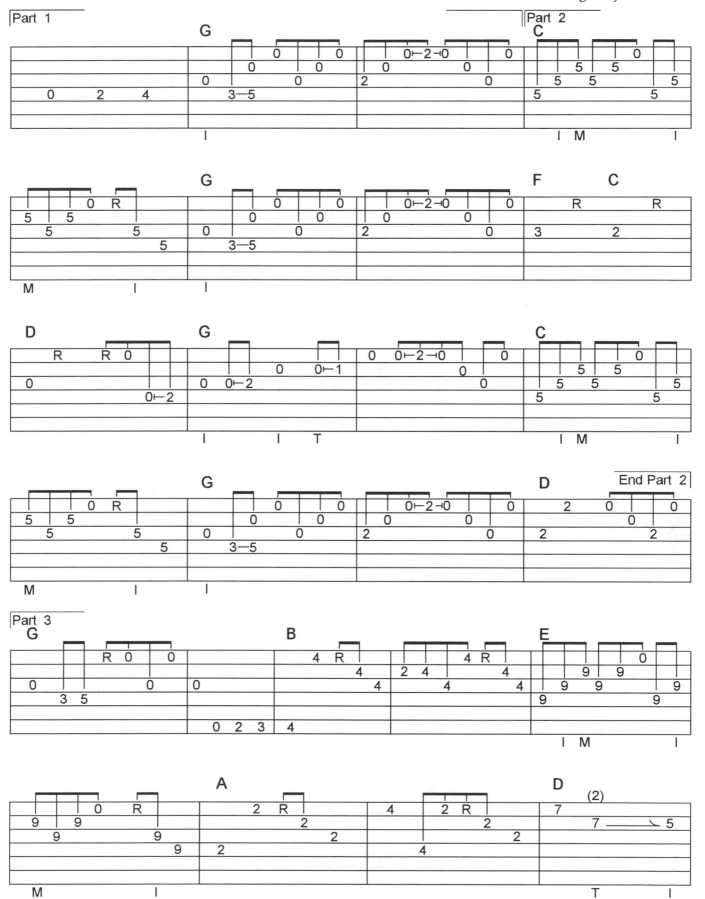

29

```
                    G                              End Part 3
        R           9 0   0 5 0   0 2 0   0     0       0
                      0       0       0
5—7           7                                     Repeat Part 2
        7                               3—2 0
        I   T M T M T M T M   T M T M
```

```
        0   0       (2)
      0         0
          2
```

No. 559—A double groove steel designed for utility and ease of execution; this type of steel, of increasing popularity, has been greatly improved by Gibson. Size: 3" x 1⅛" x ¼". Complete in leather case.
Each, $.75; Dozen, $9.00

No. 555—Very fine moderate priced hardened steel; light weight with rounded edges. Nickel plated. Size: 3⅛" x 1" x ¼".
Each, $.25; Dozen, $3.00

No. 554—Waverly steel with corrugated sides and rounded edges; a very popular steel. Size: 3¼" x 1¼" x 5/16". Each, $.50; Dozen, $5.50

Steel bars from a 1936 Gibson catalog

RED HAIRED BOY

key: G

Arranged by Steve Toth

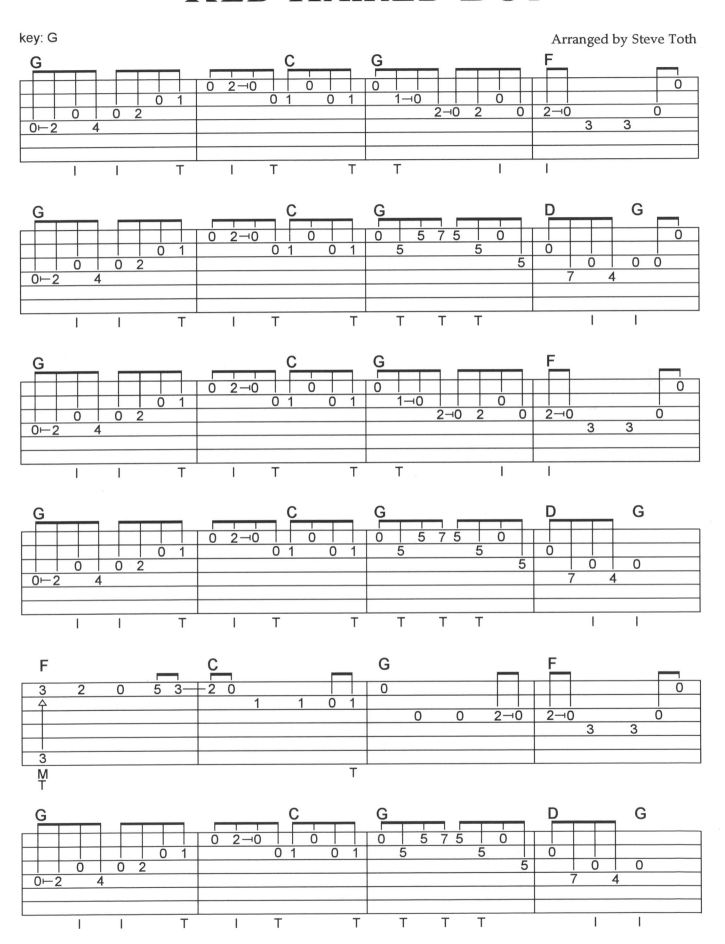

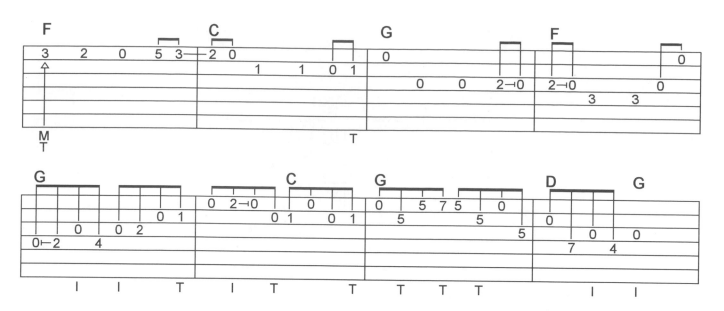

Born to play that "dobro"
3 year old Eddie Rainey.   Garfield, N.J. 1975

SALLY ANN

key: A
capo: 2

Arranged by Steve Toth

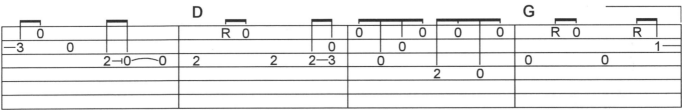

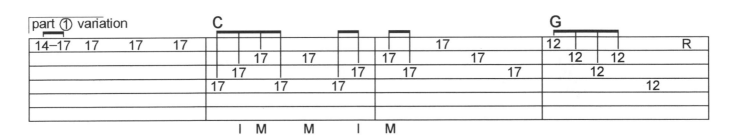

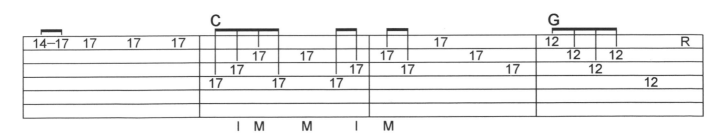

33

part ②variation   D   G

```
| 10-12  9   7 |  7  R     7  R  7-9  7        |           R            |
|         8    |  7              7     7       |    10-12        12     |
|              |                    7~7        |            12~12       |
```

```
| 10-12  9   7 |  7  R     7  R  7-9  7        |           R            |
|         8    |  7              7     7       |    10-12        12     |
|              |                    7~7        |            12          |
```

THE SOUL OF DOBRO
Patents Pending

SALLY GOODIN

key: A
capo: 2

Arranged by Steve Toth

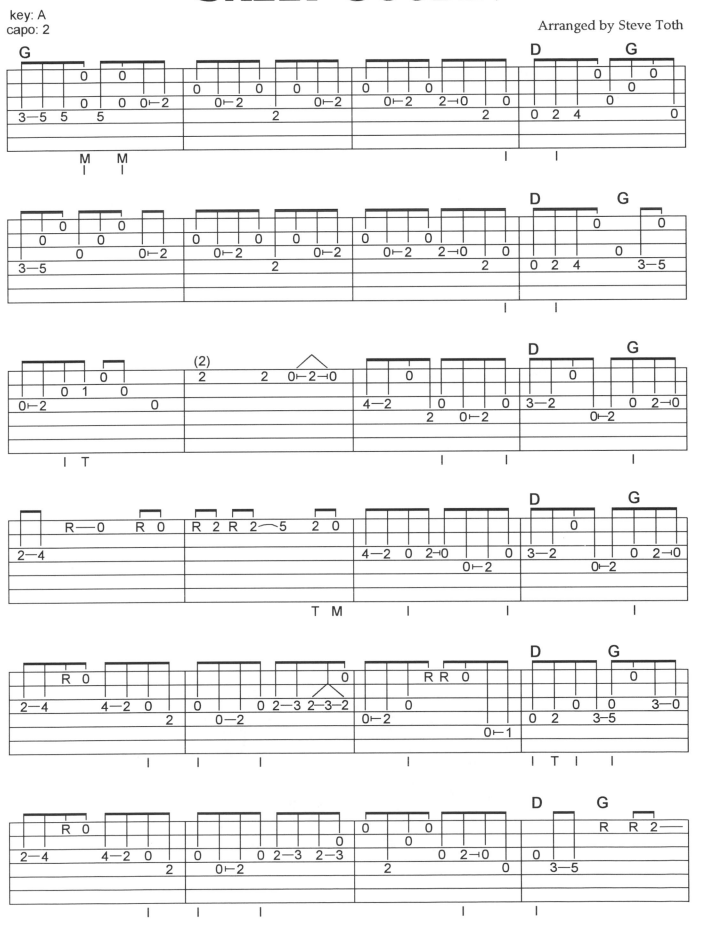

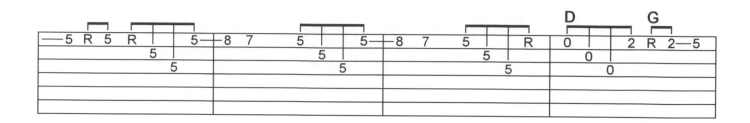

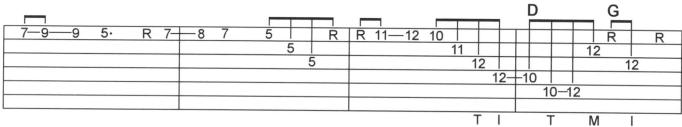

Oahu Monel Round Bars

SALT CREEK

key: G

Arranged by Steve Toth

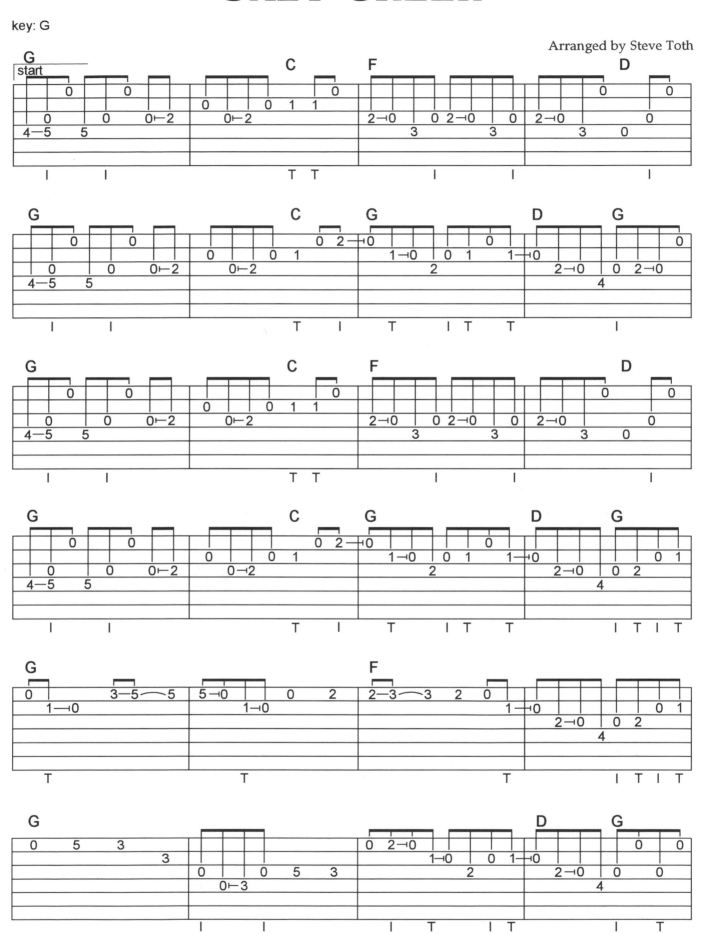

37

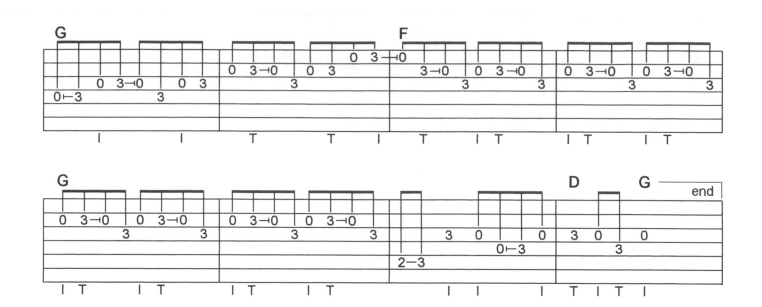

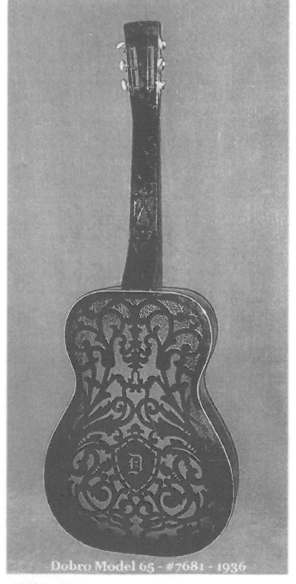

Dobro Model 65 - #7681 – 1936

SLIDING DOWN THE ROAD

key: A
capo: 2

by Steve Toth

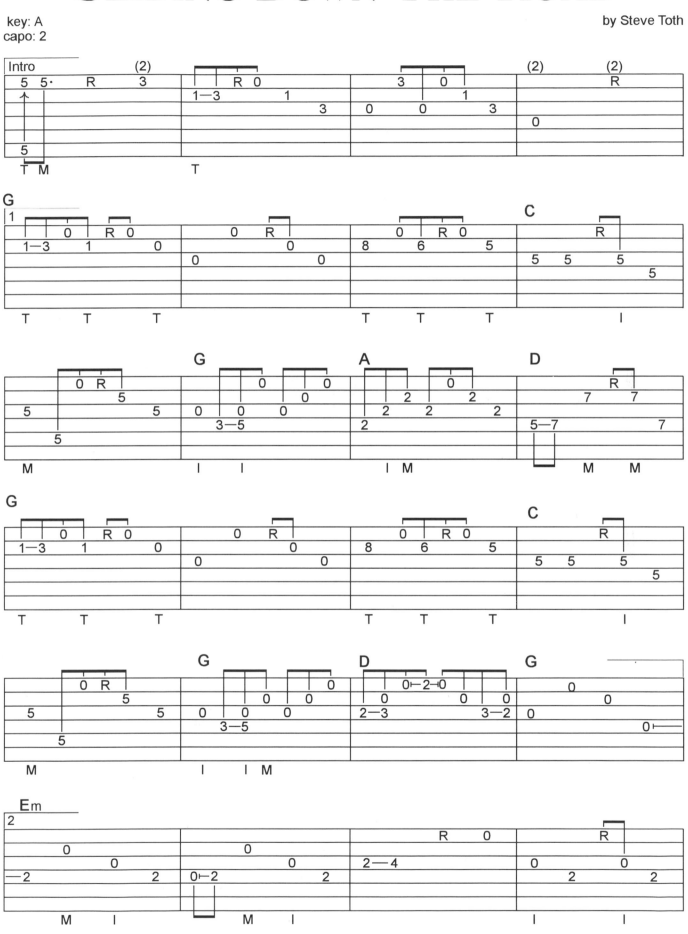

39

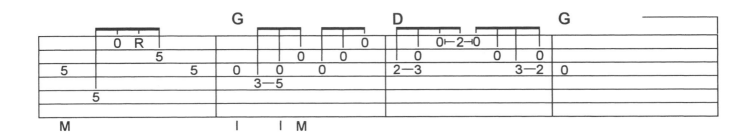

Tag (same as intro)   (2)

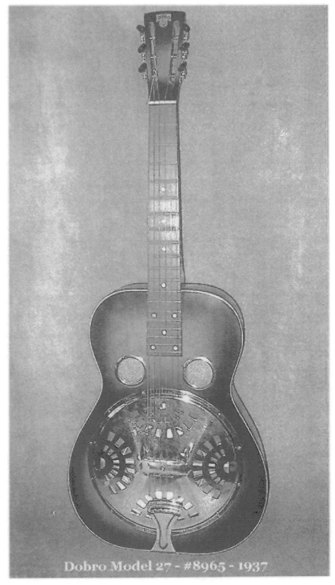

Dobro Model 37 - #7771 – 1936

Dobro Model 27 - #8965 – 1937

SOMETIMES ALONE

key: A
capo: 2

by Steve Toth

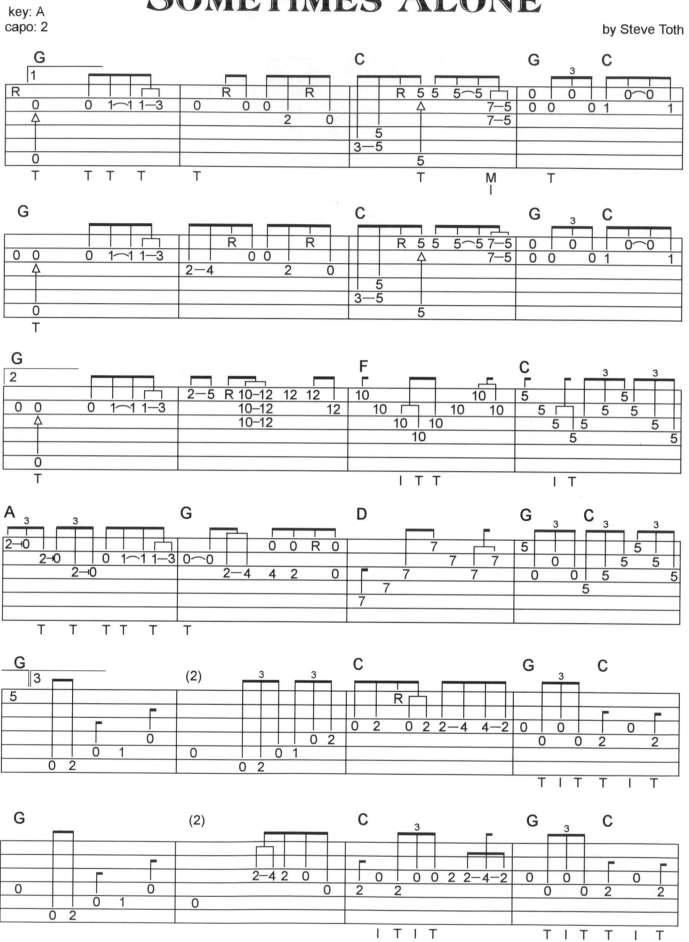

42

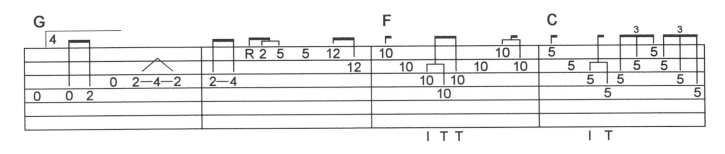

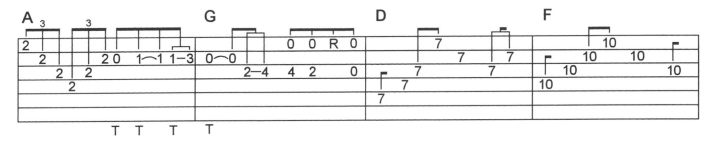

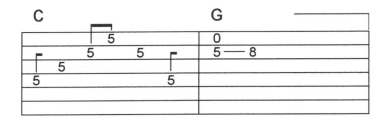

Dobro Model 45 - #8906 – 1937

Dobro Model 45 - #4101 – c1935

43

SOUTHWIND

key: A

by Steve Toth

45

Step To It

by Steve Toth

key: B
capo: 4

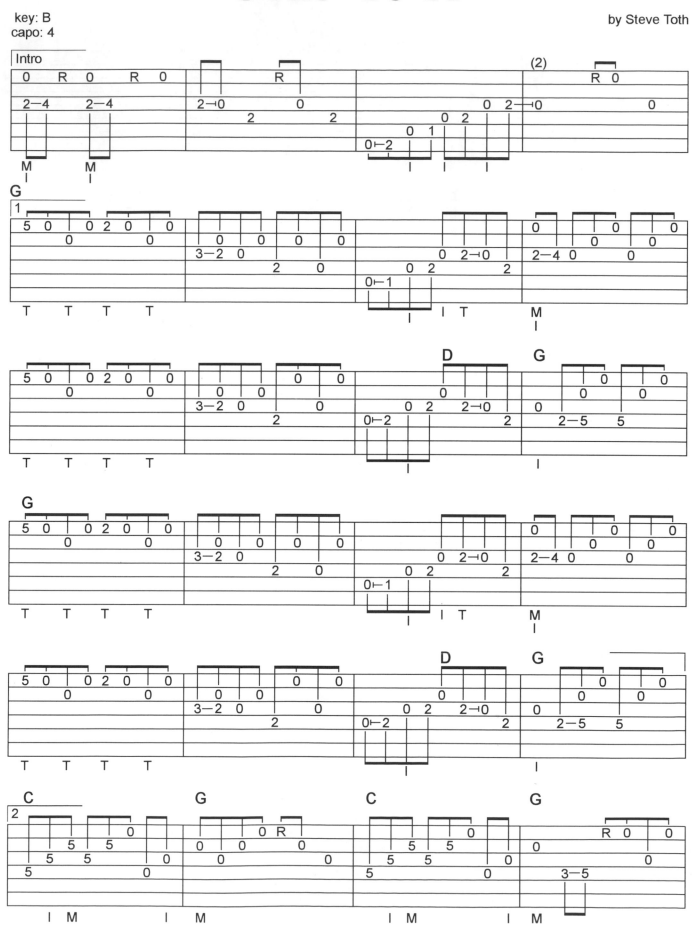

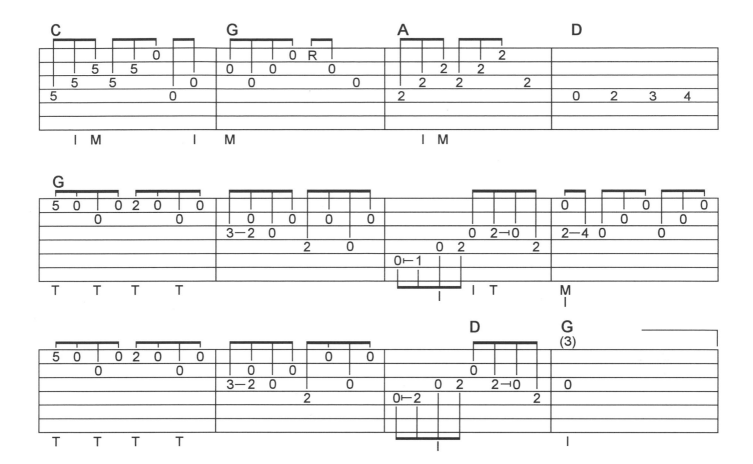

GUITAR INSTRUCTION & TECHNIQUE

GUITAR CHORDS PLUS
by Ron Middlebrook
A comprehensive study of normal and extended chords, tuning, keys, transposing, capo use, and more. Includes over 500 helpful photos and diagrams, a key to guitar symbols, and a glossary of guitar terms.
00000011...$11.95

GUITAR TUNING FOR THE COMPLETE MUSICAL IDIOT (FOR SMART PEOPLE TOO)*
by Ron Middlebrook
A complete book on how to tune up. Contents include: Everything You Need To Know About Tuning; Intonation; Strings; 12-String Tuning; Picks; and much more.
00000002 ....$5.95

INTRODUCTION TO ROOTS GUITAR

by Doug Cox
This book/CD pack by Canada's premier guitar and Dobro* player introduces beginning to intermediate players to many of the basics of folk/roots guitar. Topics covered include: basic theory, tuning, reading tablature, right- and left-hand patterns, blues rhythms, Travis picking, frailing patterns, flatpicking, open tunings, slide and many more. CD includes 40 demonstration tracks.
00000262 Book/CD Pack $17.95
00000265 VHS Video.............................$19.95

KILLER PENTATONICS FOR GUITAR*
by Dave Celentano
Covers innovative and diverse ways of playing pentatonic scales in blues, rock and heavy metal. The licks and ideas in this book will give you a fresh approach to playing the pentatonic scale, hopefully inspiring you to reach for higher levels in your playing. The 37-minute companion CD features recorded examples.
00000285 Book/CD Pack $17.95

LEFT HAND GUITAR CHORD CHART*
by Ron Middlebrook
Printed on durable card stock, this "first-of-a-kind" guitar chord chart displays all forms of major and minor chords in two forms, beginner and advanced.
00000005...$2.95

MELODIC LINES FOR THE INTERMEDIATE GUITARIST NEW
by Greg Cooper
This book/CD pack is essential for anyone interested in expanding melodic concepts on the guitar. Author Greg Cooper covers: picking exercises; major, minor, dominant and altered lines; blues and jazz turn-arounds; and more.
00000312 Book/CD Pack $19.95

MELODY CHORDS FOR GUITAR*
by Allan Holdsworth
Influential fusion player Allan Holdsworth provides guitarists with a simplified method of learning chords, in diagram form, for playing accompaniments and for playing popular melodies in "chord-solo" style. Covers: major, minor, altered, dominant and diminished scale notes in chord form, with lots of helpful reference tables and diagrams.
00000222...$19.95

MODAL JAMS AND THEORY*
by Dave Celentano
This book shows you how to play the modes, the theory behind mode construction, how to play any mode in any key, how to play the proper mode over a given chord progression, and how to write chord progressions for each of the seven modes. The CD includes two rhythm tracks and a short solo for each mode so guitarists can practice with a "real" band.
00000163 Book/CD Pack $17.95

MONSTER SCALES AND MODES*
by Dave Celentano
This book is a complete compilation of scales, modes, exotic scales, and theory. It covers the most common and exotic scales, theory on how they're constructed, and practical applications. No prior music theory knowledge is necessary, since every section is broken down and explained very clearly.
00000140...$7.95

OPEN GUITAR TUNINGS*

by Ron Middlebrook
This booklet illustrates over 75 different tunings in easy-to-read diagrams. Includes tunings used by artists such as Chet Atkins, Michael Hedges, Jimmy Page, Joe Satriani and more for rock, blues, bluegrass, folk and country styles including open D (for slide guitar), Em, open C, modal tunings and many more.
00000130...$4.95

OPEN TUNINGS FOR GUITAR*

by Dorian Michael
This book provides 14 folk songs in 9 tunings to help guitarists become comfortable with changing tunings. Songs are ordered so that changing from one tuning to another is logical and non-intrusive. Includes: Fisher Blues (DADGBE) • Fine Toast to Hewlett (DGDGBE) • George Barbazan (DGDGBD) • Amelia (DGDGCD) • Will the Circle Be Unbroken (DADF#AD) • more.
00000224 Book/CD Pack $19.95

ARRANGING FOR OPEN GUITAR TUNINGS NEW
By Dorian Michael
This book/CD pack teaches intermediate-level guitarists how to choose an appropriate tuning for a song, develop an arrangement, and solve any problems that may arise while turning a melody into a guitar piece to play and enjoy.
00000313 Book/CD Pack $19.95

ROCK RHYTHM GUITAR

by Dave Celentano
This helpful book/CD pack cuts out all the confusing technical talk and just gives guitarists the essential tools to get them playing. With Celentano's tips, anyone can build a solid foundation of basic skills to play almost any rhythm guitar style. The exercises and examples are on the CD, in order of difficulty, so players can master new techniques, then move on to more challenging material.
00000274 Book/CD Pack $17.95

SCALES AND MODES IN THE BEGINNING*
by Ron Middlebrook
The most comprehensive and complete scale book written especially for the guitar. Chapers include: Fretboard Visualization • Scale Terminology • Scales and Modes • and a Scale to Chord Guide.
00000010 ....$11.95

SLIDE GUITAR AND OPEN TUNINGS*

by Doug Cox
Explores the basics of open tunings and slide guitar for the intermediate player, including licks, chords, songs and patterns. This is not just a repertoire book, but rather an approach for guitarists to jam with others, invent their own songs, and understand how to find their way around open tunings with and without a slide. The accompanying CD features 37 tracks.
00000243 Book/CD Pack $17.95

SPEED METAL

by Dave Celentano
In an attempt to teach the aspiring rock guitarist how to pick faster and play more melodically, Dave Celentano uses heavy metal neo-classical styles from Paganini and Bach to rock in this great book/CD pack. The book is structured to take the player through the examples in order of difficulty.
00000261 Book/CD Pack $17.95

*Includes tablature